I Know Someone with a
Visual Impairment

Vic Parker

Heinemann Library
Chicago, Illinois

www.heinemannraintree.com
Visit our website to find out
more information about
Heinemann-Raintree books.

To order:
☎ Phone 888-454-2279
💻 Visit www.heinemannraintree.com
to browse our catalog and order online.

Edited by Rebecca Rissman, Dan Nunn,
   and Catherine Veitch
Designed by Steve Mead and Joanna Hinton Malivoire
Picture research by Tracy Cummins
Originated by Capstone Global Library
Printed in the United States of America by
Worzalla Publishing

14 13 12 11 10
10 9 8 7 6 5 4 3 2 1

Library of Congress Cataloging-in-Publication Data
Parker, Victoria.
  I know someone with a visual impairment / Vic Parker.
     p. cm.—(Understanding health issues)
  Includes bibliographical references and index.
  ISBN 978-1-4329-4562-6 (hc)
  ISBN 978-1-4329-4578-7 (pb)
  1. Vision disorders—Juvenile literature. 2. Blindness—
Juvenile literature. I. Title.
  RE52.P37 2011
  617.7—dc22   2010026577

Acknowledgments
We would like to thank the following for permission to
reproduce photographs: AP Photo pp. **5** (Amanda Lee
Myers/State Press Magazine), **18** (Ron Heflin); Corbis
pp. **8** (© Brooklyn Production), **10** (© Ken Seet), **24** (©
MARIO ANZUONI/Reuters); Getty Images pp. **6** (De
Agostini Picture Library/De Agostini), **11** (Superstudio),
22 (Jeff Mitchell/FIFA), **23** (Altrendo Images), **25**
(Matthew Stockman), **27** (Julia Smith); istockphoto
pp. **4** (© John Prescott), **12** (© Ken Hurst), **14** (© Rich
Legg), **16** (© PeJo29), **20** (© ericsphotography); Photo
Researchers, Inc. pp. **9** (Burger/Phanie), **13** (Pascal
Goetgheluck), **17** (Dr P. Marazzi); PhotoEdit p. **21** (©
Tony Freeman); Shutterstock p. **19** (©Karin Hildebrand
Lau).

Cover photograph of Mikaela Stevens reading braille
at the Louis Braille Center of Edmonds reproduced with
permission of AP Photo (The Herald, Dan Bates).

We would like to thank Ashley Wolinski and Matthew
Siegel for their invaluable help in the preparation of
this book.

Every effort has been made to contact copyright
holders of any material reproduced in this book. Any
omissions will be rectified in subsequent printings if
notice is given to the publisher.

All the Internet addresses (URLs) given in this book
were valid at the time of going to press. However, due
to the dynamic nature of the Internet, some addresses
may have changed, or sites may have changed or
ceased to exist since publication. While the author and
publisher regret any inconvenience this may cause
readers, no responsibility for any such changes can be
accepted by either the author or the publisher.

Contents

Some words are printed in bold, **like this**. You can find out what they mean in the glossary.

Do You Know Someone with a Visual Impairment?

We use our eyes and **brain** to see and make sense of what we see. You might have a friend with a visual **impairment**. This means he or she has problems seeing things.

You cannot catch sight problems from someone else.

A person with a severe visual impairment may use a white stick to guide them.

You might be able to tell that people have a visual impairment by looking at them. They may wear glasses. Or their eyes may not look at you directly when they talk to you.

What Is a Visual Impairment?

Light enters the eye through the small black hole at the front of it, called the pupil. It passes through a **lens** in the middle and hits the back, called the retina. Here, pictures are made of everything around us.

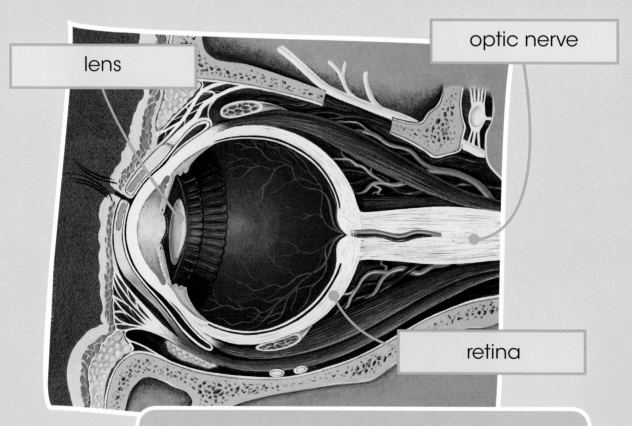

lens

optic nerve

retina

Pictures from the world around us are sent from the eye, along the **optic nerve**, to the **brain**. The brain makes sense of them.

When there is a problem with or damage to parts of this process, it can cause a visual **impairment**.

Different people can have different types of impairment:

- People may have trouble seeing things far away, close up, or at their sides.

- People may not see colors properly.

- People's sight may be blurry, shadowy, or completely dark.

- One eye or both eyes can be affected, and one eye can be worse than the other.

Testing for a Visual Impairment

There are lots of tests that can be done to check for a visual **impairment**. These can be carried out by an eye expert such as an **optician**.

An eye expert may test how well your eye is working by shining a bright light in it.

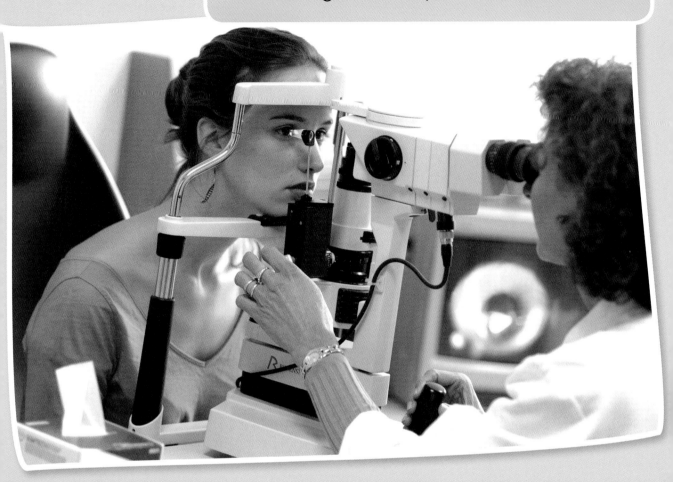

Tests for a visual impairment may feel a little strange, but they do not hurt.

When people have their eyes tested, they may look at a chart and say what they can see. They may have to cover one eye or look through different **lenses**.

Farsightedness and Nearsightedness

People can be farsighted or nearsighted. These problems are caused by parts of the eye becoming out of shape. Being farsighted means that you have problems seeing what is close to you—for example, when you are reading from a computer screen or a book.

Anyone can develop farsightedness or nearsightedness, but it often runs in families.

If left untreated, nearsightedness and farsightedness can make it difficult for you to do your best in some activities.

Being nearsighted means you have problems seeing what is far away—for example, the writing on a classroom whiteboard.

Treatments for Farsightedness and Nearsightedness

Farsightedness and nearsightedness can be helped by wearing **lenses** that make up for shape problems in the eye. You wear lenses either on your face as glasses, or directly on your eyeball as contact lenses.

Contact lenses are so tiny that you cannot tell that someone is wearing them.

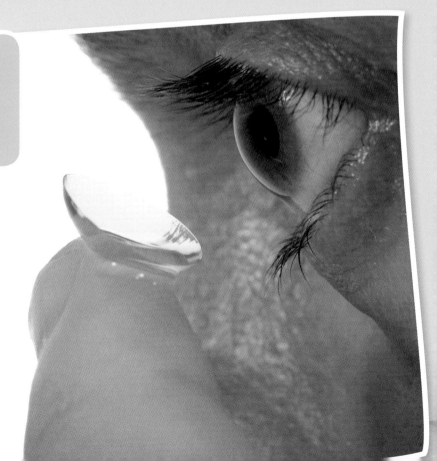

Sometimes farsightedness and nearsightedness can also be helped by an **operation**, called **laser surgery**. Laser surgery can correct a shape problem with a person's eye forever.

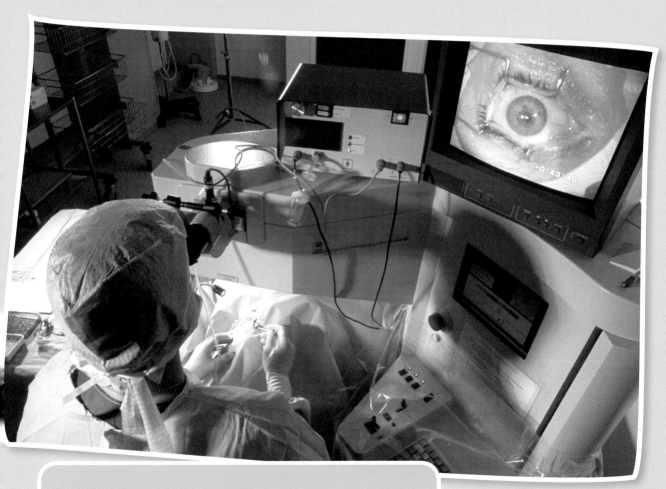

Having laser surgery usually means that a person does not have to wear glasses or contact lenses anymore.

Who Can Be Blind?

If people have a severe visual **impairment**, we say they are **partially sighted**. If people cannot see anything at all, we say they are blind.

Blind people sometimes wear dark glasses so that other people cannot see their eyes.

People can become partially sighted or blind at any time in their lives:

- Babies can be born blind.
- Children can go blind if they do not eat enough food with Vitamin A.
- People can go blind through illness or accident.
- Older people can go blind because they have eye problems that they get with age.

Treatments for Blindness

If some eye problems are caught early, a person's sight can be saved. For example, special eye drops can stop an eye problem called glaucoma from causing sight loss.

Glaucoma can cause blindness.

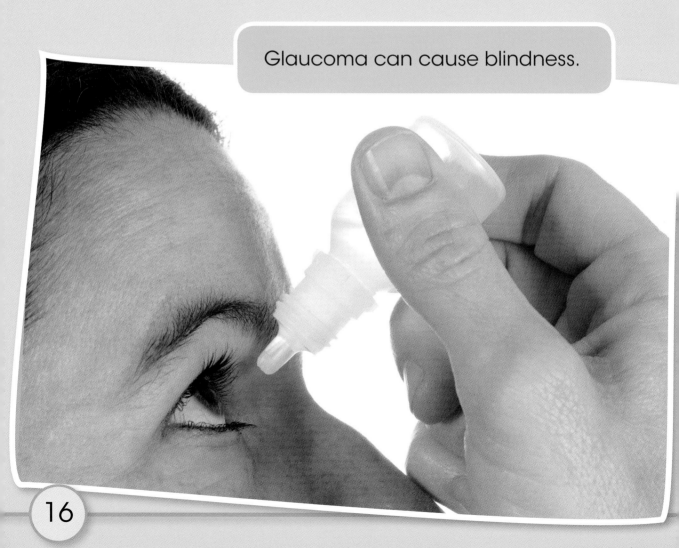

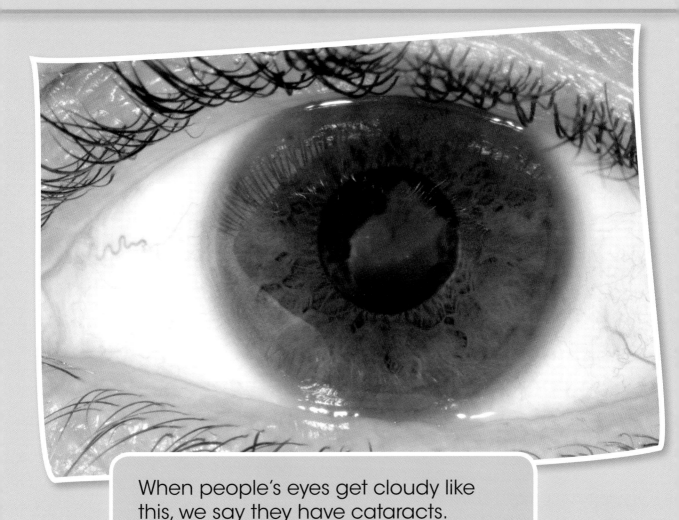

When people's eyes get cloudy like this, we say they have cataracts.

Other types of severe visual **impairment** can also be cured. For example, sometimes people's eye **lenses** can become cloudy. They can have an **operation** to replace their lenses.

Living with Blindness

A special machine can help a partially sighted person to read newspapers or books.

Many people's severe sight loss cannot be prevented or cured. These people face lots of challenges each day of their lives—for example, cooking, joining in games, crossing the road, and driving.

Severe sight loss can be very upsetting for people who could once see well. However, with the right support, **partially sighted** and blind people can live full, happy lives.

Visually impaired people can do well at most activities.

At School and College

Special learning methods can really help blind and **partially sighted** people. They can have special books that use little bumps called **Braille**. They read the Braille by running their fingers over the bumps.

Visually impaired people can use their sense of touch to help them learn.

There are also computers that can read pages of writing out loud. All these things can help children to learn at ordinary schools, or at special schools for the blind.

Visually impaired people can use their sense of hearing to help them learn at school and college.

At Home and Going Out

People with severe visual **impairments** can use computer software that reads everything on screen out loud. They can also watch television or visit the theater by listening to a description of the action through a headset.

People with severe visual impairments do not have to miss out on fun activities like going to a soccer game.

A blind person who has the help of a service dog can go out and about on their own.

Some people with severe visual impairments have service dogs to help them get around. A service dog can be trained to lead its owner around and even take the owner across the road safely.

Famous People

Stevie Wonder is a music star who has been blind since he was a baby. He has said his blindness is a good thing, because it made him concentrate on his hearing and love of music.

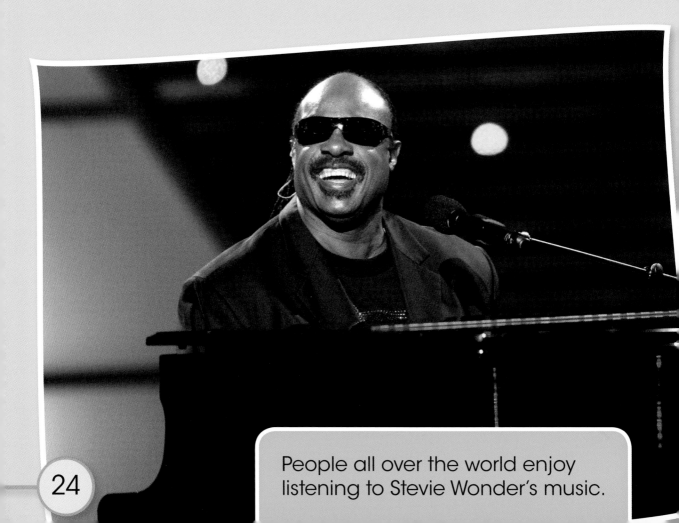

People all over the world enjoy listening to Stevie Wonder's music.

Marla Runyan can only see the markings on running tracks and roads very faintly.

Marla Runyan has been severely visually impaired since she was nine years old. This has not stopped her from becoming a champion marathon runner. She has beaten many sighted runners in top international races.

Being a Good Friend

There are many ways you can be a good friend to someone with a visual **impairment**, such as:

- wearing a blindfold for a few hours to see what living without sight is like

- offering help if your friend needs it (but let your friend help you sometimes, too)

- looking directly at your friend when you speak to him or her, just as you would with others.

Living with a visual impairment can be difficult at times. But there are many other ways we are all different. A good friend likes us just as we are.

We all have different bodies and personalities.

Visual Impairments: Facts and Fiction

Facts

- About 10 million Americans have visual **impairments**.

- Visually impaired people can get talking clocks to help them know what time it is.

- A visually impaired person who carries a white stick with red bands on, or has a service dog with red bands on its harness, has a hearing impairment, too.

Fiction

(?) People with severe visual impairments need lots of extra help at school and work.

> **WRONG!** They need different help from sighted people, not more.

(?) It is OK to pet a service dog.

> **WRONG!** Service dogs are working dogs and should not be distracted. You should ask the owner first if you want to pet it.

(?) Blind people can often hear or smell better than others.

> **WRONG!** Blind people are not naturally stronger in their other senses than sighted people. However, they can work to improve their other senses.

Glossary

Braille writing system for blind people. It uses raised dots that blind people can feel.

brain body part inside your skull that controls all other parts of your body and that helps you to think

impairment condition that stops part of your body from working correctly

laser surgery operation in which a doctor uses a strong beam of light to change the shape of the eye

lens piece of curved glass or other clear material that helps people to see. You have a lens in your eye.

operation type of medical treatment carried out in a hospital by a doctor called a surgeon

optician expert who tests your eyesight

optic nerve part of the body that carries pictures from the eye to the brain

partially sighted has trouble seeing